JACK LENTINI &
THE PIRATE QUEEN
PETER HUGHES

Newton-le-Willows

Published in the United Kingdom in 2024
by The Knives Forks And Spoons Press,
51 Pipit Avenue,
Newton-le-Willows,
Merseyside,
WA12 9RG.

ISBN 978-1-916590-08-3

Copyright © Peter Hughes 2024.

The right of Peter Hughes to be identified as the author of this work has been asserted by them in accordance with the Copyrights, Designs and Patents Act of 1988. All rights reserved. No part of this publication may be reproduced, stored in a retrieval system, transmitted in any form or by any means, electronic, photocopying, recording or otherwise, without prior permission of the publisher.

Acknowledgements:

Thanks to Kirah Van Sickle for artwork and cover design.

Thanks to Giacomo, Eliana, Eugenio and Lola for Sicilian, Neapolitan and Umbrian sustenance.

'I couldn't let go of the sonnet
Look how out of hand it's gotten'

– Stephen Sanchez

for KPQ

Giacomo da Lentini

Giacomo da Lentini was a Sicilian poet who probably wrote the very first sonnets. He was a notary at the court of Frederick II in Palermo in the early years of the 13th century. Sicily, in that period, was already multicultural with scholars, philosophers, scientists and artists from the Christian, Judaic and Muslim traditions sharing thoughts and insights. Giacomo absorbs and reworks the Occitan traditions and poetic forms of southern France into local modes and procedures. Interestingly there is no trace of his original 'Sicilian' texts. We have only the transcriptions into Tuscan. So, translation and adjustment, not to mention gentrification, is there in the poetry from the start.

Periplo – A Prelude

    the magic lamp appears to work
warm breath & strokes translate me
    while they tinker with the clock-hands
        on the town's medieval tower
& harvest this year's olives from the sky

    the genie swapped my spirit beast
    for the pup of the pirate queen
      the girl who set a course for dawn
    then gently rearranged my mouth

    she's off to circumnavigate the island
      & paint the way the wake unwinds
    past shifting bays & headlands
see if she can find a new location
      to park the boat & come ashore

1

    chilies once plucked
from the bush
  hanging upside down
      from the beam in the kitchen ceiling
         by the woman in the cowgirl hat
           & little else
              are fucking wonderful

  kennst du das Land
wo die Citroën
        veered off the highway
    into a valley of olives
      & vines inside my heart
        say six hours east
            of Carolina

2

      it is 1225 in Palermo
the moonlight falling through December
   theory & the window
      won't be breaking anything but hearts
         the Christmas lights are coming on
     along the main streets & piazza

     they say love grills a couple of hearts
          on a single shish-kebab stick
   but Jesus it's feeling so late in the day
    & the moon is playing a *cor anglais*
       through a small glass jar of tears
     the kind they used to bury with the dead

3

        every continental philosopher
        was wondering how she could fit
                through my eyes
let alone be carted around in my heart
 well I just sat down in Umbria
   one sunny late-May morning
     my back against an olive tree
          & something else took root

      the pirate queen is checking her agenda
running a salty forefinger haltingly down my chart
  butt dialling the harbour-master
  tending a pot of basil on the poop deck
in which my severed head is nurturing
   her aromatic leaves beneath the swaying stars

Peter Hughes

4

an unbelievably deep blue Advent
sky is chanting over Spello
& olive trees are doing those impressions
of transcendence
I still don't understand
which parts of me are functioning
it's hot and cold in different corners
of the terrace

some of us are reading books
on post-traumatic stress
the left and right sides still not talking
as her sloop puts in to the dodgy
car-boot dockside of Palermo
everything goes everywhere

5

she paddles through blue shallows & reflections
with Puff Diddy – a new pet puffer fish
who can't get the hang of swimming to heel
or retrieving the pirate's tossed olives
not that the Pirate Queen could give a damn
as she exposes her wind-rose tattoo
to the prevailing winds & constellations

& remembers the Umbrian shadows
where *whisperedtoheldtightcaressed&fucked*
became our temporary password
nothing has ever been so easy to remember
such Peruvian cuisine in sweet alignment
with the personable music of her spheres
& nights of Irish pipes & baccalà

6

    winters of Tuscan bean stew & chianti
remember not to talk about her
  sideways glance towards the future perfect
    misunderstood Sicilian tercets
      the late night scents of omertà & jasmine
      hear the trumpet raga cross the waters
    where she's moored out in the straights

    of course I adore her unregistered sloop
      informal crew & booty
    we won't know till tomorrow
     if she'll be setting out
        from Wilmington
       from Charleston
     or Savannah

7

    one idea for the title was Jack Lentini
       & the Pirate Queen on Ice
       another was Jack Lentini
    & the Pirate Queen – Berth of the Cool
we nearly went with LENT but that was taken

    after another week of circular breathing
& pirate pilates we binged on
    Jon Hassell & all of the possible musics
       & 4th world sounds & echoes
    then became contenders – so many pop-up cribs
       tucked into the alleys of the hill town
           where each star left its clothes

Peter Hughes

8

once you'd gifted me the old brass lamp
& after snacks & disambiguation
& after a bottle or two
of whatever was reflected
in your eyes
& southern windows
we rearranged the layers of perception

moored the fading day to stars
slipped down over the side of the boat
to stroke the moonlight
dive for pearls
go down
throughout the night
the heavens

9

      the one in which Jack said he likes her face
fourteen times & I say yes well so do I
  but what about poetics
    what about her buckles & techniques
      her earthquake-management hacks
        her knack of straddling in boots

     all wilting in the skip of my imagination
   she drives all day through Far Away
then parks outside some dusty chandlers
on a rusting edge of northern Cackalacky

    I follow the advice – I'm breathing in & out
this mental collection of fake portraits
  one upon the others will keep trembling into
    new configurations – just press play

Peter Hughes

10

    her face her face her face her face (Part Two)
I'm also bigging up
    her wine red octopus-on-acid hair
        which does the seaweed thing across her breasts
            & down her back & did I mention
        her shoulders no because I was thinking
      about her hair still & how it sways &
      whispers to my loins & eyelashes

    I need to scooch & swivel to address
      the subject properly
        O my America! my newfoundland
      have I even talked about her butt yet
    probably not – you would have remembered
      p.s. her face her face her face her face

11

      the Pirate Queen relaxes at the helm
    of an old Toyota pick up truck – grey hues
so nearly equidistant between Pastel & Bone
              between Naples & Bonita Springs
     the train I ride has crossed the Thames or Tiber
      followed the trail of the lonesome pine

    or wandrin' star – I knock back my last glass
of Shotover Prospect at the back bar of the King's Arms
   & head through the parks towards my fields
  the relentless hissing of the sky above the Cherwell
    do not forget
              this may be the glider's final flight
    the last guided tour of the cavern

      & still I'd love to drive the calves with you

Peter Hughes

12

love songs dip & flutter
on these breezes from Assisi
sounds like Radio Subasio
with subtle scents of mint under the wings
rise over the aqueduct trail up the mountain

the jury's still out as to whether
or to what extent a modern English line
or vintage Sicilian smoothied into Tuscan
could register the glances sweat & yearn
throughout the kind of dance that saw us
turn & duck out of the hall into these
deep tree shadows where we're kissing hard
against the bark & where your long red hair
is still wrapped tight around my fingers

13

    it's one of those days
  when you know in your heart
      that the time has come
    to earthquake-proof the outhouse
reading room & sensibility
the ground has moved too often
    swinging & tilting my dreams &
meditations as to whether Carolina
  (North) is really 1800 badgers wide

          🍎

here come the lead & rubber bearings
    the diagonal braces are unpacked
her sequestered schooner bangs against the quay
    about 3.20 Wednesday afternoon

Peter Hughes

14

because you're hot
& bright I veer towards you
in the night
not very much like a moth
towards a toaster
to be honest   your face
one for luck   your mouth
& what it postulates

resilience & sportive equilibrium or Sagrantino
& those aquamarine streaks on Spanish leather
your undulating take upon the nocturne
the flapping signal flags between your masts
the way you leaf through all the paperwork
& collage in a portal

15

    if you'd never seen a flame
you might say wow
      such warm & shiny dancing air
          let's breathe & eat some   damn
        you wouldn't have a clue as to how
  it burns life into agonising embers

      god I hate metaphors
look
    by all means toast marshmallows
        on the bonfire of your choice
      but maybe leave her out of it
we're having a night in
  uncork the wine put on some Doors
    hum along to come on baby light my fire

16

      let me count the ways
      she is not like a diamond
        ruby or saxophone solo
          or ham on a plinth
        or the latest Milanese collections

unless you have the company of one
  who changes who you are
    so as to reincorporate the world
      which touches you again all
        over while you blink in morning blackbird
          light with stupid joyful fear packed in your throat

17

    I wonder if the troubadours
    & trobairitz are really that concerned
    with inaccessibility & garden centres
      some say that she outshines the sun
    but they mostly live in Berkshire

    the world is constant rearrangement
    of the figurative & abstract
      of worn-out topcoats & supports
    of inconsistent & evolving presences
& possibilities that too few still believe in
potential throbbing through the night
the diesel on the far side of the park hums on
    her barrel of lime fingers is despatched
      & on its way from Sicily

18

    the Pirate Queen hangs out more flags
    to flap another message through the breeze
    with Sin & Des – her parrots of the Caribbean
        she's expecting every man to do his duty
            including Hook who puts the birds to bed
                with a litter picker & a baseball mitt
            the signal resounded & reopened
    an absence in the sky & time lassoed

        then wrens & blackbirds in shivering timbers
        & a spunky little treecreeper spiralling back up
        the warm & textured bark of the sestet
            before vanishing into edera & heart
        the flag text may have said the time to drink
        the best wine in the house & hold is now

19

    the pirates are getting out their squeezeboxes
    & fictitious instruments which have been
        imperfectly maintained to be honest
          they like to accompany imagined whale-song
      while knocking back the lime & ginger rum
until they're lying down & jamming deck jazz
  as are we all of course we want to buy
    our friends one more scotch egg or passport

        to eternity but must make do with one last
  pint of Guinness – ah two! – with maybe
    one last cheese & onion quaver there's no
chance of one more *cwtch* or kiss my friend
    the wind will carry us away in French
      Sicilian or Tuscan no matter who plays on

20

there's no final song as the sequence
is extended through these misunderstandings
counterfeit archaeological knock-offs
booths retailing fake Etruscan verse & vases
tenzoni from the eastern seaboard
Ted Berrigan & Bernadette Mayer
Terrance Hayes & Cavalcanti
out on the decking just shooting the shit

comparing their virtual voltas & exchanging
bitter observations on the state of the nations
the Pirate Queen is sketching mast & wake
she says you have to run your flags
& grow your runner beans up something

21

    the pirate queen & I are back
on the same boat & boy it's rocking
       I consult her face her face
& ease the tiller half a span to port
we scrape against the dockside
  then clatter down the gangplank
      & head into the bar for a grechetto

    we're opening a little jar
     of last year's light & capers
a hint of island flugelhorn
  drifts down through certain alleys
       from the principle piazza
    she turns to me
        adjusts my mouth & stars

Peter Hughes

Postlude – Periplo

    a hint of moonlight through the blinds
   the blended scent of hair & thyme
    through painted clouds white orchids
nestle their faces in a song of burnt sienna
her voice recalls the blossom of the south
 & firm oranges still attached & sun-warmed squeeze
   their juice into these lines & tumblers

the background hums with strokes & text
unspecified developments & tendril growth
or early musical notation which brings us up
   to date & never speaks of never though it often
    tastes of cinnamon acrylic paint & Aperol
with blowtorched peel & just beyond the wall
   you hear & feel the swifts returning

Some Notes on the Sonnets

1. Giacomo uses the image of a lily dying as soon as it is picked to represent the devastation he feels on separation from his lady. I am thinking more about food, olives, grapes and sex. Goethe makes a guest appearance in the sestet. Readers of his *Erotica Romana* will recall that the great German poet also had little enthusiasm for the unplucked.

2. Giacomo observes that light can pass through glass without shattering it and a glimpse of his beloved whizzes through his eyeballs without any obvious surface damage. The havoc takes place deeper in and out of sight. Love melts and reforms the two lovers into one sweet sweaty Italianate situation and this is even more uncomfortable and memorable than it sounds.

3. The original poem wonders, somewhat disingenuously, how this adult woman can squeeze through his tiny eyeballs on the way to starting all those forest fires beneath his ribs. She's summer sun and his eyes are just two more empty bottles irresponsibly discarded in dry bracken. Attentive readers will already have noted that there are fewer pirates in Lentini than in these recent versions. But French fashions had to cross the waters somehow and it may have been through blues guitar and New Orleans.

4. This afternoon I wasn't in the mood to deal with love psychosis.

5. In his poem Giacomo is getting fed up with the lady's nonchalant detachment. I, with one eye on possible film rights, provide a picturesque Caribbean interlude – as well as kitchen tips and soundtrack hints.

6. This sonnet refreshingly concerns keeping your mouth shut.

7. Sometimes the weather turns and you end up meditating on nomenclature and jazz.

8. Giacomo persuades himself that loving this woman is exactly what God would have wanted. I add that an old wardrobe is not the only way into Narnia. There's also the SS3.

9. In his sonnet Giacomo really does keep saying *face face face* while insisting that hers is the finest ever seen. I pour another glass of Trebbiano Spoletino and allow my mind and hands to wander.

10. In this poem Giacomo continues to celebrate the outstanding beauty of her face while I riff on some of her other attributes with a little nod to Donne.

11. Giacomo speaks of distance, contrasts, the mobile and the static, the delicate and stony. Naples FL and Naples are about 5,350 miles apart.

12. The original reflects upon the possible benefits of patience and so should we all.

13. Giacomo's talk of how powerful rulers should be cruel to be kind tastes sour in a period featuring such luminaries as Netanyahu, Putin and Trump. We're also plagued by earthquakes and environmental degradation. If anyone has any information about badgers as a unit of measurement I'd be glad to hear more. Some evenings wild mushroom risotto is not the best choice on the menu.

14. This poem is about the foolish things we do in the name of love, art and misread signals, not to mention culinary fusion.

15. My poem is disturbingly close to the original. Although, I slightly sweeten Giacomo's grumbling in the sestet. I now realise he was correct.

16. Giacomo lists all the precious stones that are less beautiful than his lady. He praises her virtue. I have a panic attack. Fortunately the Sicilian Bar is still open.

17. Giacomo's version of Perfect is just as annoying as Ed Sheeran's. Although, to be fair, the Sicilian's claim that God could never do a better job is bold.

18. It is hard to imagine nowadays how original it would have been for Giacomo to say that there must be an angel playing with his heart. And in case you are wondering about the names of the Pirate Queen's parrots, Sin and Des, well they're just nicknames.

Sin usually sits on her left shoulder, Des on the right. Sinistra and Destra was too much of a mouthful. Also, *carpe diem*, of course.

19. Sophie Hunger's version of *Le vent nous portera* is perhaps my favourite. I have lost a lot of friends along the way because of fatal restlessness and a strong desire to preempt named storms. I'm sorry.

20. Do people still write essays on authenticity and poetic influence? Are such works still collected by university presses in slim volumes and sold for a sum greater than most people are able to spend on food for a month for their entire families? Are the writers still unpaid, but told it will be good for their cv?

21. This is a poem of affection and consummation – gratitude for one more unpredictable day. Research students and others will be interested to learn that Giacomo now runs the Sicilian Bar in via Roma.

22. The swifts really have returned. They animate the dusk above my terrace. Take care everyone.

www.ingramcontent.com/pod-product-compliance
Lightning Source LLC
Chambersburg PA
CBHW011958060426
42444CB00046B/3460